JBIOG
Moss
Stewart, Mark

Randy Moss : first in flight

football's new wave

Randy Moss

First in Flight

By
Mark Stewart

THE MILLBROOK PRESS
BROOKFIELD, CONNECTICUT

M

THE MILLBROOK PRESS

Produced by
BITTERSWEET PUBLISHING
John Sammis, President
and
TEAM STEWART, INC.

Series Design and Electronic Page Makeup by
JAFFE ENTERPRISES
Ron Jaffe

Researched and Edited by Mariah Morgan

All photos courtesy
AP/ Wide World Photos, Inc.
except the following:
SportsChrome, Steve Woltmann — Cover
The Charleston Gazette — Pages 6, 7, 9 top, 9 bottom, 11, 19, 20
The following images are from the collection of Team Stewart:
ESPN Magazine, ESPN, Inc. (1998) — Page 40
Peterson Publishing Co., LLC (1999) — Page 47

Printed in the United States of America

Published by

The Millbrook Press, Inc.
2 Old New Milford Road
Brookfield, Connecticut   06804

Visit us at our Web site – http://www.millbrookpress.com

Library of Congress Cataloging-in-Publication Data

Stewart, Mark.
   Randy Moss: first in flight / by Mark Stewart
   p.   cm.   — (Football's new wave)
   Includes index.
   Summary: A biography of the Minnesota Vikings wide receiver, Randy Moss, highlighting his on-field skills and the off-field controversy that has surrounded him.
   ISBN 0-7613-1518-7 (lib. bdg.)   ISBN 0-7613-1333-8 (pbk.)
   1. Moss, Randy—Juvenile literature. 2. Football players—United States—Biography—Juvenile literature. [1. Moss, Randy. 2. Football players. 3. Afro-Americans Biography.] I. Title. II. Series.
GV939.M67S84   2000
796.332'092—dc21
[B]   99-34796
                                                                                 CIP

pbk: 1 3 5 7 9 10 8 6 4 2
lib: 1 3 5 7 9 10 8 6 4 2

Contents

High Hopes, Hard Lessons

chapter

"Ever since I was a young boy, I've dreamed of playing in the NFL."
— RANDY MOSS

For more than a century, the mining region around the West Virginia capital of Charleston has furnished the United States with much of the raw energy it has needed to grow. The people who live and work in these areas are tough and proud. They put down strong roots, and they have big dreams. Some, like Randy Moss, dream of a life beyond the state's borders and use their toughness and pride to carve out a career in sports.

Randy grew up in the town of Rand, a collection of a few hundred tiny homes next to a chemical factory in the Kanawha Valley, near Charleston. His mother, Maxine, was a single parent who was determined to raise her son right. She made sure Randy went to church at least three times a week, and she did not allow any kind of foul language or alcohol in her home.

As the NFL's top young receiver, Randy Moss has the world at his fingertips. It was not always that way, however.

*The DuPont plant in Belle dominated the landscape of Randy's early life.
He walked past it every day on the way to school.*

Work in towns like Rand was hard to come by, and did not pay very well, so Maxine often worked two shifts a day as a nurse's aide to make ends meet. She wanted to spend more time with Randy, but could not afford to. But she believed that she had raised him to be a good, responsible child, and that he would be able to fend for himself and avoid trouble when she was not there to look after him.

As a rule, Randy did stay out of trouble. He paid attention in school and spent much of his free time playing sports. He was much better than the other boys his age, and he liked the way that made him feel. He even began to think he might be a professional athlete some day.

Although Randy never lived with his father, he did not lack role models. He had a half-brother named Eric, who was two years older. Eric was quite an achiever. He was a good student and respected leader, and was student council president one year. Eric also was a star on his football and basketball teams from grade school right through high school. He earned All-State honors in hoops and honorable mention as an All-American in football. Randy's first introduction to football, in fact, came when he carried Eric's equipment to midget-league games. "*He* was a star," Randy says of Eric. "I just wanted people to *notice* me."

Of course, Randy's biggest inspiration was his mother. When he became old enough to understand how hard his mom worked, he began to get very serious about his dream of playing pro sports. Sometimes, after enduring a 20-hour day, Maxine would drag herself into the house, collapse on her bed, and simply pass out. It broke Randy's heart. He vowed to her that, one day, he would make sure she never had to work again.

> ## Did You Know?
>
> Before Randy came along, the biggest sports star in West Virginia history was Olympic gold medalist and NBA Hall of Famer Jerry West. "Mr. Clutch" led East Bank High School to the state championship in 1956, and took the University of West Virginia to the NCAA final in 1959.

> "I come from a strong family. I didn't feel anything could stop the Moss family."
> **RANDY MOSS**

Superstar in the Spotlight

chapter **1**

"If he had signed to go to West Virginia, his penalties and punishments wouldn't have been as severe. I hate to say that about the place where I live, but it's true."
— CHARLESTON BUSINESSMAN TONY GORDON

Rand does not have a school of its own. Technically, it is unincorporated, which means it is not really a town at all. So every morning, the children of Rand walk past the DuPont factory and into the neighboring town of Belle. It has been that way for as long as anyone can remember. And as long as anyone can remember, Belle (which is populated mostly by white families) has not been thrilled about sharing its educational facilities with Rand (which has a large number of African-American residents). Complicating this matter is the fact that many of the children who attend the schools in Belle come from the surrounding hills and hollows, where they rarely encounter people of color.

Over the years, there have been a few racial incidents, but mostly the black kids and white kids stay out of each other's way. The 40 or so black students at DuPont High School, for instance, just kind of blend into the background. Unfortunately, this was not an option for Randy, who enrolled at DuPont in the fall of 1991. When you are

DuPont High School

more than six feet tall, and can run faster and jump higher than anyone else in the state, it is hard to lose yourself in the crowd.

Randy was already well known the day he set foot on campus. In local youth leagues and in pickup games, he had distinguished himself as a tremendous basketball and baseball player. Randy also was one of the best all-around football players in the area. To some at DuPont, this made him a hero. To others, however, it made him a target.

There was one area of the school nicknamed "Red Neck Alley." It was a section of hallway populated by white students who made no secret of their hatred of blacks. Their lockers there were decorated with Confederate flags and Ku Klux Klan symbols. The boys in Red Neck Alley often directed their anger at Randy, calling him names and even threatening him. Randy remembered the lessons he had learned in church—the lessons of tolerance and love and forgiveness—but at times he felt like challenging them all to a fight. "There was a lot of racism going on all the time," remembers Randy. "I didn't know how to handle it."

Luckily, Randy could take out his frustration on some of these same boys on the football field, where he played both offense and defense. As a receiver, he used his size and speed in different ways against

Randy is congratulated by fans after a TD catch in the 1992 state championship game.

different defenders. Against smaller, lighter opponents, Randy would crash into them after the snap and send them sprawling. Against larger, less mobile defenders, he would bust a move and leave them stumbling to catch up. If he was double-teamed, he could outjostle and outjump the defensive backs. And if a ball was thrown behind him, he could reach back and grab it without even breaking stride. On defense, Randy never met a receiver he could not completely take out of a game.

By his senior year, Randy was the most celebrated athlete in the state. He had great balance and tremendous footwork, a 41-inch vertical leap, and big, soft hands. This not only made him West Virginia Football Player of the Year in 1994, but it also made him the state's top basketball player as a junior *and* senior. Indeed, NBA scouts who watched Randy insist he would have been a star in the NBA.

Randy's athletic exploits also included a year as DuPont's star center fielder and a couple of weeks with the track team during the spring of his sophomore year. That same year, his half-brother, Eric, was being scouted by several big-time football programs. A large, physical athlete who could play the line, catch passes, and run the football, Eric eventually accepted a scholarship from Ohio State University. This was extremely encouraging for Randy, who was by this time considered the more talented of the two Moss boys. It seemed as if his future in the game would be secure. "In high school, I knew I'd make it big," admits Randy.

After Randy led his team to the 1994 football state championship, his name was at the top of nearly every college recruiting list—in both football and basketball. He accepted an offer to play for the Notre Dame football team. You cannot find a better program in college sports, and the education the school offers is first-rate in every way. All Randy had to do was get through his last semester of school, keep his grades up, and stay out of trouble.

But at DuPont High, trouble always seemed to be down the corridor. Randy's choice to leave the state (Notre Dame is located in Indiana) did not make him popular with many of his class-

> *"Randy Moss was the greatest high school football player I ever saw. Nobody close. It was like watching a man play against boys."*
> LOU HOLTZ, FORMER NOTRE DAME COACH

Randy watches game tape with members of the DuPont coaching staff.

mates. They had hoped he would attend the University of West Virginia. His decision to attend Notre Dame was seen as a rejection of the region that had produced him.

Compounding Randy's troubles was the fact that he had been dating a white girl named Libby Offut. By his senior year, they had already produced a child, a girl named Sydney. Although Randy and Libby were in love—and are still together—those who felt that people of different races should not mix were enraged by this relationship.

Randy's locker was just down the hall from Red Neck Alley, and as his senior year progressed, the threats and taunts became more intense. Finally, in March, everything came to a head. A boy from Red Neck Alley challenged one of Randy's friends to a fight. He asked Randy to back him up, in case the one-on-one battle turned into something bigger. Randy agreed, and watched as his friend beat up the other boy. Suddenly, Randy jumped in and kicked him twice while he was down. To this day he does not know what came over him. "In a fight, you don't think," he says. "It was just like my temper took over—like I was another person."

The police were summoned and everyone pointed at Randy; he was arrested and later booked for assault. Because he had just turned 18, Randy was charged as an adult. Because he was a famous athlete who had "turned his back" on West Virginia, he suddenly found the system working against him. His picture was in the newspaper and on television. The local prosecutor, perhaps hoping to make a name for himself, refused to give Randy the customary slap on the wrist and pressed hard for a conviction. Eventually, Randy had to plead guilty.

Suddenly, everything Randy had worked for and dreamed of began to unravel. He was expelled from DuPont. Notre Dame canceled his scholarship. And he was sentenced to 30 days in jail, plus probation.

A Second Chance

chapter }

"Every scrimmage he caught a touchdown."
— FLORIDA STATE UNIVERSITY
RECEIVER ANDRE COOPER

Although Notre Dame was no longer in the cards for Randy, the team's coach, Lou Holtz, was still in his corner. He liked Randy, and knew there was a lot more to the story than what he read in the papers. Technically, Notre Dame had rescinded Randy's scholarship because he failed to score high enough on an academic test, so Holtz's hands were tied. But he was able to help Randy get into another school with a great football team. Holtz phoned his friend, coach Bobby Bowden of Florida State University, and told him that Randy was a good kid. He explained that Randy had been caught in a tough political situation, and encouraged Bowden to offer him a scholarship.

Bowden knew all about Randy. He had recruited him, and Florida State was among the final schools on Randy's list before he selected Notre Dame. Bowden contacted Randy and told him he could join the Seminoles if he agreed to sit out a year. Several

*Randy poses proudly in front of the Seminole logo after arriving at the
Florida State campus in August of 1995. He agreed to red-shirt the 1995 season,*

No one at FSU had ever seen an athlete with Randy's combination of size, speed, and skill. Randy could hardly wait to suit up for the 1996 season.

FSU players had gotten into trouble recently, he explained, and bringing in a freshman with a police record might cause more controversy. Randy had no problem with this arrangement.

Bowden had an excellent track record when it came to producing NFL-caliber players, and that was Randy's ultimate goal. He joined a team that included standouts Pete Boulware, Warrick Dunn, Tra Thomas, Reinard Wilson, Clay Shiver, Danny Kanell, and Andre Wadsworth. "I consider Florida State as getting you ready for the NFL," Randy said at the time. He was right. Every one of the aforementioned players ended up in the pros.

Randy began to make his mark when spring practice began in 1996. He proved right away that he was ready to assume a major role in the Florida State offense. Some who watched him claimed he was the best Seminole freshman ever. No one could cover him—no one even wanted to try. Bowden and his coaching staff could not wait to see what Randy did against their opponents the following fall.

Even though he had not played a single down, everyone on campus knew who Randy was. It felt great to be wanted. As the semester ended and Randy prepared to head back to West Virginia for the summer, everyone wished him luck. They should have wished him common sense.

The Moss File

RANDY'S FAVORITE...

Music Group . . . . 8 Ball
Rap Artist . . . . Master P
Nickname . . . . "Dawg"—that's what he calls all of his teammates
Contest . . . . Slam Dunking
Fantasy . . . . Making the Olympic track team
Activity . . . . Doing normal stuff. "I go home, play with my kids, go to bed, get up, and go to work."

Randy and Libby now have two kids: Sydney and Thaddeus.

Did You Know?

During his red-shirt season at Florida State, Randy was timed at 4.25 seconds in the 40-yard dash. That is absolutely amazing for a man his size. The fastest time ever recorded at FSU was 4.23, by Deion Sanders, who stood 4 inches shorter and weighed 25 pounds less than Randy.

Up in Smoke

chapter 4

"What was I thinking?
Nothing, obviously."
— RANDY MOSS

When you are 19, famous, and riding high, it seems like nothing can harm you. When Randy got home, all he had to do was keep cool, stay out of trouble, and finish serving his time from the 1995 assault conviction. He would attend West Virginia State, a local college, during the day, then return to jail for the night. Just a few weeks, and he would be in the clear. A couple of days before reporting to jail, Randy was celebrating with friends when he encountered a foe he could not outrun or outjump: his own stupidity.

Someone passed Randy a marijuana cig-

"He runs like a scalded dog."
FLORIDA STATE COACH
BOBBY BOWDEN

arette. Without thinking, he took a couple of puffs and then passed it along. Randy did not do drugs. In fact, he was not *allowed* to—he knew he could be tested at any time, and if any illegal substances were found in his system, the consequences would be severe. Randy quickly came to his senses, but it was too late. "I was really being dumb, just hanging out," he says. "It was something I shouldn't have done, and I paid the price."

Two days later he was tested, and the results came back positive. When Coach Bowden found out, he cancelled Randy's scholarship. His probation was revoked, and 90 days of additional jail time was tacked on to his sentence. "Jail was the lowest," Randy says. "Jail was a place where you get your mind right."

All Randy ever wanted to do was play football. Now, thanks to two brief moments of poor judgment, he was a football outcast. No Division I program in the country would touch him with a ten-foot pole.

While Randy stewed in his jail cell that summer, he formulated a plan to salvage his career. One of the assistants at Florida State, Bob Pruett, was now the head coach at Marshall University, a Division I-AA school in West Virginia. He contacted the coach, explained his situation, and asked if there was a spot for him on the team. Pruett had liked Randy at FSU. He told Randy he could join the Thundering Herd, but warned him that this would likely be his final opportunity to play football. No more brawls, no more drugs, no more controversy. This was just the break Randy needed. The football players at the Division I-AA level are good, but not great. Typically, they are former high-school stars who lack the size or the speed or the raw talent that major-college football programs seek out. Against this competition, Randy could dominate.

Marshall already had a solid team; Randy's presence in the Thundering Herd's 1996 lineup made them unbeatable. Opponents had to double- and triple-team Randy, which opened up the field for the rest of the offense. And despite this extra attention, Randy flourished. In the season opener, he made three touchdown grabs against West Virginia State. He got two more in the second week against Georgia Southern. Randy caught one TD in each in the next three contests, then hauled in two against both Western Carolina and Appalachian State. After seven weeks, Marshall had not come close to losing a game, and Randy was within range of several NCAA records.

In Randy's eighth college game, he broke loose for four touchdown catches against The Citadel. Then he scored touchdowns in his next two games to close out the regular season with a total of 19—more than any freshman receiver in the history of college football.

But the season was not over. In Division I-AA, the top teams meet in a playoff series to determine the national "small-school" championship. As the competition got better, so did Randy. Against Delaware in the first round, he scored three times and amassed a school-record 288 receiving yards. In the next game, against Furman, he scored twice more. In the national semifinals, against Northern Iowa, Randy made yet another touchdown catch. Finally, in the Division I-AA title game, Randy completely dominated the University of Montana, with

Did You Know?

After the Division I-AA title game, Montana's Athletic Director sent Florida State coach Bobby Bowden a note saying that if he had not kicked Randy off the team, they would both be national champions!

nine catches for 220 yards and four touchdowns. He also took a handoff and ran for a 32-yard score. Marshall had its championship, and Randy was the game's most talked-about receiver.

Randy scored a total of 28 touchdowns for the Thundering Herd in 1996, tying a Division I-AA record set by all-time great Jerry Rice. This was both a great honor and a weird coincidence. Many nights during the year, Randy and his roommate would pass

Randy is mobbed by fans after Marshall wins the 1996 Division I-AA championship against Montana. He set an NCAA record for receiving yards by a freshman that year, with 1,074.

the time watching highlight films of Rice. Randy also set an NCAA mark for freshmen with 1,074 receiving yards. Teams not only had to cover Randy when they were on defense, but they also had to deal with him whenever they kicked the ball. He returned punts for the Thundering Herd, and also played deep on kickoffs. Despite the fact that most opponents purposely kicked the ball *away* from him, Randy still ran back 18 balls for 612 yards, leading all college players with an average of 34 yards per return.

Back to the Big Time

"Two summers ago, I was sitting in jail wondering if I'd ever get another chance. Now they're talking about the Heisman."

— **RANDY MOSS**

andy took a big step back into the college football mainstream when Marshall was promoted to Division I and accepted into the Mid-America Conference for 1997. This meant he would face better defenders and, more important, smarter coaches. They would devise defenses specifically to stop Randy. It would be a great challenge, an ideal chance, to showcase his skills. This was important to Randy, because he had decided by this point to enter the NFL draft as soon as he could. He knew he was already as good as many pro receivers, and wanted to leave the college game at the end of the season.

Division I here I come! Randy did not miss a beat after Marshall was admitted to the Mid-America Conference in 1997.

> "Moss is the greatest wide receiver since Jerry Rice."
> LEGENDARY COACH BILL WALSH

The defensive backs he played against in 1997 knew this, too. In fact, many relished the chance to cover him because they could gauge instantly whether or not they had the talent to move on to the NFL. If you could stay with Randy for a game, you could stay with anyone.

In Randy's first Division I game, the season opener against West Virginia, he was spectacular. Battling double coverage all day, he still managed to catch seven balls and score a pair of touchdowns. A week later, against Army, Randy scored touchdowns on plays of 79 and 90 yards. Against Kent State in the season's third week, he racked up over 200 receiving yards and scored three TDs. In week four, he scored twice more against Western Illinois. Obviously, the move to Division I had hardly slowed Randy down. Against Ball State, he and quarterback Chad Pennington connected for five touchdown passes to set a school record.

Over the next six games, Randy hauled in eight more scoring passes. In the Mid-Atlantic Conference championship game, against Toledo, he caught seven balls

Did You Know?

Randy agreed to run track for Marshall as a sophomore and won the Southern Conference indoor track 55- and 200-meter championships. He had not raced competitively for four years, yet his time in the 200 (21.15) was one of the best in the country that year. "He has greatness written all over him," Marshall track coach Jeff Small said of Randy. "He could be as good as (Olympic sprinter) Michael Johnson."

for two scores as Marshall took the title. On December 26, in the Motor City Bowl, he capped off a great year with six catches and a breathtaking 80-yard touchdown in a win over Mississippi.

Randy finished the 1997 season with the Mid-America Conference records for receiving yards and touchdown catches. His 25 touchdowns eclipsed the all-time Division I record. He also won the Biletnikoff Award as the nation's best receiver. And when it came time to vote for the Heisman Trophy—the ultimate honor in college foot-

Rarely has there been a closer race for the Heisman Trophy than in 1997. Randy is flanked by quarterbacks Peyton Manning and Ryan Leaf. The winner, Charles Woodson, stands at far left.

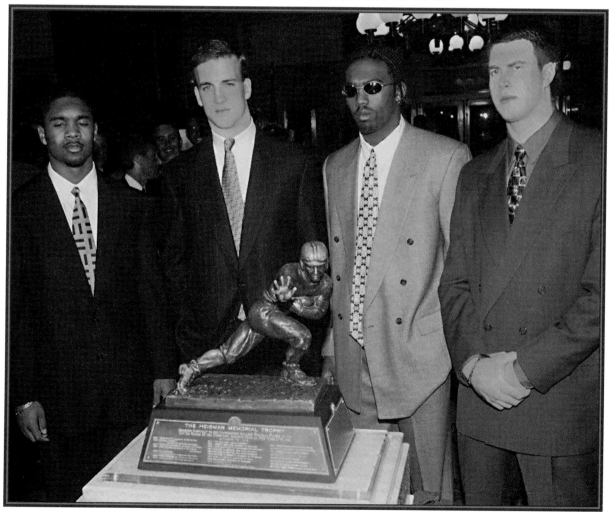

ball—Randy was one of the top choices. He finished fourth, but the winner, Charles Woodson of Michigan, admitted Randy probably deserved it. Many believed that the fact that Randy did not attend a famous "football school" prevented him from winning the Heisman.

After two college seasons, Randy had amassed unbelievable statistics. He had 168 receptions and 53 TD catches. Between his catches, runs, and returns, he had 4,528 yards. Had Randy stayed and played his final two seasons—and merely maintained the same pace—there is little doubt that he would have established new NCAA records for receptions, touchdowns, receiving yards, and points scored. But Randy was not on the four-year plan. "All I wanted out of college was to get to the next level," he admits.

college *stats*

Year	School	Catches	Yards	Yards/Catch	Long	TDs
1995	Florida St.	Red-Shirted—Did Not Play				
1996	Marshall	78	1,709	21.9	80	28
1997	Marshall	96	1,820	18.6	90	26
Total		**174**	**3,529**	**20.3**		**54**

college *highlights*

First-Team All-American . . . . .1996 & 1997
Fourth in Heisman Trophy voting 1997
Biletnikoff Award winner 1997
Mid-America Conference Player of the Year 1997
All-Southern Conference 1996
Division I-AA Offensive Player of the Year 1996
TD Catches in Record 11 Straight Game 1996
NCAA Kick Return Leader 1996

We Love Randy, But...

chapter 6

> "Moss is the most intriguing player in the draft because he has the potential to be the best pick...and the worst."
>
> — DAN POMPEI, SPORTSWRITER

Getting to the next level would not be as easy as Randy thought. Thanks to an incident in the fall of 1997, his judgment and maturity again came into question. Randy and Libby were discussing their daughter, Sydney. What started as a difference of opinion turned into a heated argument, and unfortunately the argument spilled outside in front of Libby's house, in full view of the neighbors. Someone called the police and reported a domestic dispute. When the patrol car arrived, the officers saw Libby push Randy

> "Our scouts say he's the best receiver to come out of college in the last 30 years."
>
> DAVE WANNSTEDT, BEARS COACH

"I saw this kid's love for the game. I knew he knew he was walking a thin line. His passion to play football would keep him out of trouble."
VIKINGS COACH DENNIS GREEN

and Randy push back. Both knew that this was no way to settle things, but they never dreamed it would land them in serious trouble.

Recognizing Randy, the officers decided to arrest him—even though Libby told them there was no problem. Then they arrested Libby! Randy and Libby were cuffed and charged them with domestic battery, despite the fact that neither wished to file a complaint against the other. Had it been any other couple, nothing would have come of the incident. No one got hurt, everyone apologized, and no damage was done. But when Randy and Libby went before a judge, the police made it sound more serious than it was. The charges would stand.

To many NFL teams, this was "strike three" for Randy. Rather than examining each incident for what it really was, all they saw was a kid who had stomped someone, been caught with drugs, and beaten the mother of his child.

Some teams, however, kept an open mind. They sent representatives to visit Randy on the Marshall campus to determine for themselves whether or not he had put his troubles behind him. No one questioned his ability or football intelligence, but they needed to know whether he was mature enough to cope with life in the National Football League.

Those who spent time with Randy were impressed. He handled himself well in interviews and did well in workouts. He was assured by scouts that he would one day be a star, and that they would definitely draft him if he was still available when their teams picked. *Finally*, Randy thought, a chance to start clean. A chance to be his own man. An opportunity to let his talent flow and let everyone see the real Randy Moss.

Unfortunately, Randy had to skip the NFL combine, where the best college players come to show their stuff. He was suffering from an abscessed wisdom tooth and needed complicated surgery. While the entire pro football world was gathered in

Indianapolis, Randy was getting six teeth pulled. Some whispered that Randy had skipped the combine because he did not want to take a drug test. At that point, most teams simply drew a line through his name. Spending millions on this kid was simply too risky.

Randy, meanwhile, was unaware that he had been written off. On draft day, he was prepared to be one of the first players picked. Then he watched in dismay as he slid down the chart—*way* down the chart. Nineteen teams passed on him, including the Bengals, who had two chances to grab him and turned him down twice. Randy was particularly upset when the Cowboys let him go. He loved Dallas and really wanted to play for them. "Those twenty picks that went by," says Randy, "I know it was because of the character issue, and that hurts. But a lot of those teams didn't even bother to talk to me. I just wanted an opportunity to play football. That other stuff was long over."

Waiting for Randy with the 21st pick were the Minnesota Vikings. They also had their reservations about him, but they had decided to do a little digging before they gave him a thumb's-down.

Prior to the draft, team representatives spoke with Randy's friends and some others who had known him in West Virginia. They also interviewed Eric Moss, who had made the team's practice squad as a tackle in November

Did You Know?

Miami coach Jimmy Johnson would have loved to draft Randy to play with quarterback Dan Marino. Convinced Randy would not be available at number 19, he traded the pick prior to the draft!

of 1997 and was signed for 1998. As team officials suspected, Randy was just an overgrown kid who had made a couple of childish mistakes. Given his great talent, the Vikings determined he might be worth a first-round pick.

Before that decision was made, the Vikings needed to look inward. They had to be sure that they could provide an environment where Randy might mature and thrive. The Minnesota organization already had two great veteran receivers, Jake Reed and Cris Carter, as well as a talented runner named Robert Smith. That meant that Randy would not have to do it all on the field right away. He could watch and learn, and work his way into the lineup slowly. The quarterback situation was good, too. Starter Brad Johnson was regarded as one of the NFL's smartest young passers, and the backup, veteran Randall Cunningham, would be a good teacher for Randy, too. He had a reputation for working well with young receivers. Cunningham had been laying tile the year

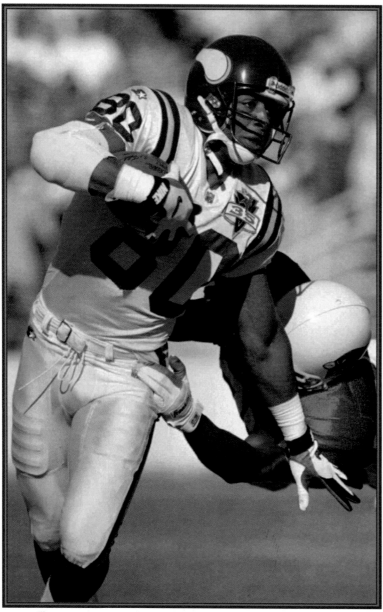

The presence of star receivers Jake Reed and Cris Carter (above) meant Randy could develop at his own pace with the Vikings.

before, having retired from the NFL. He was enticed to return to pro football by the Vikings, because he liked the team's personnel, both on the field and off. In his prime, with the Philadelphia Eagles, Cunningham had been an MVP. Slower afoot now, he could still throw the bomb as well as anyone in the league.

Coach Dennis Green would also be a big plus. One of the NFL's few African-American head coaches, he was sensitive to the needs of players like Randy. A generation earlier, he had grown up in a similar environment, endured the same struggles, and fought the same battles. Also, his passion for the game burned as intensely as Randy's. Green had no doubt that, if the Vikings were lucky enough to get the young receiver, he would devote himself completely to playing football.

There was just one more hurdle to clear. Before the draft began, Coach Green called Carter, the Vikings' team leader. Green informed him that Minnesota was ready to take Randy in the draft, but wanted to know if Carter had any objections. Carter's response? "Dream on!" There was no way 19 teams would pass on the guy.

On draft day, Carter sat dumbfounded as team after team skipped over Randy. He practically jumped for joy when the Vikings got him.

Randy, however, was not jumping for joy. By slipping so far down in the first round, he probably had lost between four and five million dollars. He looked at the Vikings' 1998 scheduled and saw that 10 of the teams that had let him go would have to face him that year. He decided he would make them pay. Then he put the whole draft behind him. Randy was happy to be in the NFL, pleased to join a team like the Vikings, and anxious to begin his pro career.

Young fans took to Randy right away. They do not know or care about his past, they just want his autograph!

chapter 1 Carter Country

"My job is to try to make him into the best receiver in the NFL."

— CRIS CARTER

Randy had done his homework on his new teammate, Cris Carter. He knew that he was one of the league's top all-time receivers, and that he was one of the most respected and well-liked players in all of football. Randy also knew that Carter had gone through his share of troubles as a young man. In college, Carter had become embroiled in an illegal agent scandal, and had lied to a grand jury during the investigation. Later, after turning pro, he had been caught using drugs and was promptly drummed out of the league. The Vikings, convinced that he was

Old-timers insist that the player whose style most resembles Randy's is Lance Alworth, the San Diego Chargers' Hall of Fame receiver of the 1960s. Like Randy, Alworth could outrun and outjump defenders, and specialized in pulling down long passes.

Long before they got to training camp, Cris Carter and Randy had become close friends. The time they spent together at Carter's home in Florida changed Randy's life.

ready to clean up his act and turn his life around, picked him up for $100. Now, Carter is almost assured of a spot in the Hall of Fame. Whatever Cris had done, reasoned Randy, it was working. Who better to seek out?

Right after the draft, Randy phoned Carter at his Florida home and asked if it would be all right to come hang out with him. This impressed Carter. He knew Randy was reaching out and asking for help. There was little Carter could show Randy on a foot-

ball field. But off the field, there was a big, mysterious world waiting for the rookie.

When Randy arrived, he joined Carter and Jake Reed in daily workouts, supervised by a personal trainer they had hired. Randy was blown away by how hard these superstars pushed themselves in the off-season. He also got to see how Carter, a young millionaire, lived his life. Money and fame bring with them responsibility. A lot of kids who sign big contracts think they can go right out and do anything they want, Carter explained, when just the opposite is true. He showed Randy you can get a lot of satisfaction from life by living smart and thinking about the future. If Randy wanted to have fun and party, that was fine, Carter said. But there is a right time and place to do it. The veteran also showed Randy how to do simple things, such as getting set up with bank accounts, doing laundry, and picking up stuff at the grocery store. "He has a good heart and a good head," says Randy of Carter. "He's a special person."

For his part, Carter was amazed at how hard Randy worked out, even though he did not have to. He was already in great shape. Carter's older brother, Butch, had played college and pro basketball, so he had been around big guys who could jump. Cris

Randy was assigned number 18 when he joined the Vikings. He switched to 84 when the regular season began.

Randy's presence in the Minnesota passing attack meant Cris Carter (above) could concentrate on running his specialty: short, precise routes that often resulted in touchdowns.

claimed that Randy was the smoothest, most coordinated, best-jumping big man he had ever seen, and predicted Randy would be the first great receiver of the 21st century.

Carter also spotted something special in the rookie—something he could not quite put his finger on. It went beyond confidence and coolness. It was a strange peacefulness that he did not expect to find in a young man with such a turbulent past. Later, Cunningham noticed the same thing. He described it as a combination of innocence, a lack of worry, and "no fear of failure."

Recognizing
Randy

*Minnesota's new star has already developed
his own NFL "cheering section."*

*"He is truly a great competitor.
That is what I like best about him."*
COACH DENNIS GREEN

*"He adjusts to the ball in the air better
than anyone I've ever seen."*
ALL-PRO REGGIE WHITE

*"He does all those little things—he
looks like he has been playing in the
league for five or six years."*
TV ANNOUNCER JOHN MADDEN

*"He's like Tom Sawyer. He gets in a lot
of trouble, but he's a good person."*
ARIZONA STAR ANDRE WADSWORTH

*"The kid's a fighter.
He knows exactly who he is."*
TEAMMATE JERRY BALL

Training Camp

"This is a great kid who just made some dumb mistakes. Credit the vikings for figuring it out."

— FRANK OFFUT, LIBBY'S DAD

When training camp started that summer, Randy was glad to see that for once he was not the center of attention. The media was focusing on a number of other issues: the Vikings were up for sale; Coach Green's job might not be secure; and there was concern about the Vikings' defense, which had allowed too many passing yards and touchdowns in 1997. The good news was that, despite a shaky defense, Minnesota had made the playoffs. Most experts agreed that a little improvement might take the team a long way.

The first day of scrimmages, Randy went up to the quarterbacks and told them that, if they saw him running even with a cornerback, that he was merely playing with him. "Just throw it far and I'll catch up," he announced. "Don't ever worry about overthrowing me." Normally, NFL quarterbacks would have laughed Randy off as a boastful rookie. But they saw that Randy was dead serious—his confidence was as impressive as his talent.

Randy's performance in camp pleased Coach Green right from the start. Early on, the Vikings scheduled a two-session scrimmage against the New Orleans Saints, and

Randy burned them for six touchdowns. Green knew he had a player who could contribute right away. This was an important development, because the coach liked to use three receivers at the same time and—until Randy arrived—he had been forced to use Chris Carter for sideline routes. Now, with Randy setting up outside, he could position Carter in the "slot" between the offensive line and the wide receiver, where he could run his specialty: short, precise routes with a high probability of success.

As far as "problems" were concerned, the only one Randy caused was with the quarterbacks. He got down the field so quickly that they were constantly underthrowing him. Johnson and Cunningham actually had to readjust their timing to get Randy the ball in stride. And even when they did not, Randy often saved the play. In an August exhibition game against the Carolina Panthers, he streaked downfield for a long bomb, but Johnson badly underthrew him. The Panther defensive back, thinking he was all alone, settled underneath the errant pass for what he thought was an easy interception. Out of nowhere came Randy, running back toward the line of scrimmage—in a blur of purple and gold, he plucked the ball out of the air for a clean catch and a big first down. The reception was replayed on television all week long.

The rest of the preseason went pretty much the same way. Randy caught a 44-yard touchdown pass in his first exhibition contest, and finished with 14 receptions for 223 yards and four scores as the Vikings went 4–0. Randy proved especially good at dealing with opponents. Figuring from his reputation that Randy had a short fuse, they did everything they could to provoke him, from insulting him to yanking his face mask when the referee was not looking. Each time, Randy just turned and walked away. No tough talk, no boasting, no in-your-face stuff. Football was his job now. And he had no interest in getting fired.

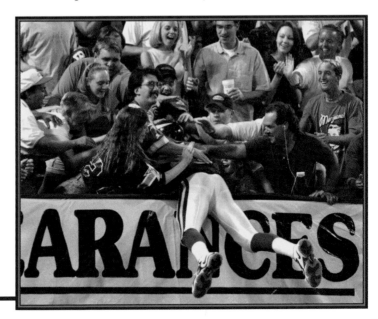

Randy is embraced by fans after one of his four preseason touchdowns.

Practically Perfect

chapter 9

*"I'm not a star.
A star is 'The Man.'
I'm not The Man on this team."*

— RANDY MOSS

When the 1998 season began, Randy was still a minor story in Minnesota. The Vikings, who had been for sale, were purchased in August by a man named Red McCombs. Many thought he would fire Coach Green, who had a reputation for speaking his mind and defying ownership. At first, McCombs said he would use the 1998 campaign to "evaluate" Green, which would have put tremendous pressure on the coach. But as McCombs got to know his players, he was struck by their deep respect for Green. On the eve of the season, McCombs decided to give him a three-year contract extension.

The players celebrated this turn of events by thrashing their opening-day opponents, the Tampa Bay Buccaneers, by a score of 31–7. The Bucs were no

"He's in a system that plays to his strengths. Minnesota has so many offensive weapons that you can't concentrate on stopping him."
TONY DUNGY, TAMPA BAY COACH

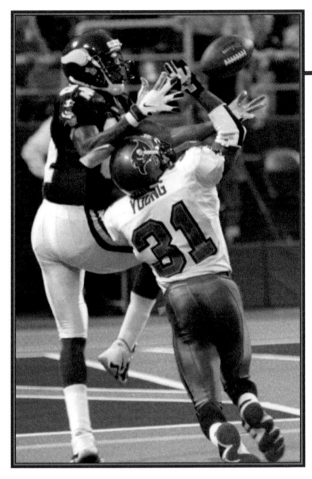

Randy's first NFL TD came on a remarkable play against Tampa Bay safety Floyd Young.

pushovers. They had an aggressive defense, a punishing running game, and one of the cagiest coaches in football, Tony Dungy. But the Minnesota offense was simply too much to handle. Randy, playing primarily on passing downs, hooked up with Brad Johnson for four long receptions and scored a pair of touchdowns.

The Tampa Bay defensive backs were completely intimidated by Randy's size. Normally, a rookie will get beat up coming off the line—veterans will test him to see how tough he is, and the referees will look the other way. It is sort of an NFL initiation. On this day, however, Randy— now 6' 4" and 200 pounds—was doing most of the initiating. When the Buccaneer defenders saw him up close, they backed off and gave him plenty of space.

Randy's first professional touchdown came on a remarkable play. Johnson underthrew him slightly, making him twist back for the ball, and giving the defensive back a clean shot at an interception. Randy reached out with his long arm, bumped the ball in the air volleyball-style past his befuddled opponent, then grabbed it as it came toward him and rolled into the end zone.

In the season's second game, Randy showed that he could do the "grunt work" that few star receivers are willing to do. Often, when a pass catcher's number is not called, he will simply go through the motions and simply try to run his man away from the play. Not Randy. On three occasions he delivered crushing blocks in crucial situations.

Talk about turning your life around! In 1996, Randy was posing for mug shots. In 1998, he was on magazine covers.

And each time, a teammate ran through the lane Randy created for a touchdown. The Vikings needed each one of those scores, too, because the Rams played them tough. Minnesota barely survived, 38–31.

One Viking who did not survive this game was Brad Johnson, who broke his leg. Randall Cunningham would now be the starting quarterback. This would make Randy even more important to the offense. Because Cunningham could throw long, Randy would be asked to streak down the field on almost every play in order to "stretch" the defense and create room for Cunningham to operate in the middle of the field.

Over the next three games, the rookie and the veteran connected for four touchdowns in victories over the Lions, Bears, and Packers. The two worked the "fade pass" to perfection, making it the NFL's most dangerous offensive play. Cunningham would wait for Randy to get between his man and the sideline and then throw the ball high and to the outside. If executed correctly, this pass could not be defended. Either Randy caught it or it floated harmlessly out of bounds.

Meanwhile, Randy was making the evening highlight shows almost every Sunday. In the Bears game, he looked like Michael Jordan as he elevated above a group of Chicago defenders and hung in the air to pull down the game-winning TD on an "alley-oop" toss from Cunningham. In the Packers game, the Vikings sent a message to the league by trouncing the defending NFC champions at Green Bay's Lambeau Field on ABC's *Monday Night Football*. A nationwide audience watched in awe as Randy made the Packers look silly. He caught five passes for 190 yards and two touchdowns, leading Minnesota to a 37–24 win. Randy's most interesting game came the following week, against the Washington Redskins. The 'Skins put veteran speedster Darrell Green on him, and the two dueled all day long. Green limited Randy to five catches, but came away extremely impressed. Besides his obvious talent, observed Green, Randy had tremendous heart.

The Vikings won three of their next four games, with Randy catching at least one pass in each. The team was looking great. Running back Robert Smith was having the best year of his career, the offensive line was superb, and the defense was holding together better than anyone had anticipated. The Vikings were blowing some teams out, but also winning the close ones. Cunningham, meanwhile, was putting up MVP numbers. In his younger days, he had tried to make things happen all by himself. Now, he was using all the tools at his disposal. The Vikings were gobbling up yardage and scoring at a record pace. No one knew how to handle them—not even the mighty Packers, who lost 28–14 in a return engagement at the Metrodome. Once again, Randy tortured the Pack, catching eight balls for 153 yards, including a 49-yard touchdown.

The second win over the Packers enabled the Vikings to wrap up the Central Division title. It also established Randy as a true "big-game" performer. In two crucial victories against Green Bay, he had hauled in 13 passes for 343 yards and three touchdowns.

Did You Know?

Randy can tell when quarterback Randall Cunningham is having trouble thinking of a play. That is when he tells him to throw it high and throw it far. "Sometimes he listens," laughs Randy, "and sometimes he doesn't." The two connected for 15 regular-season scores in 1998.

"The addition of Randy Moss made Minnesota the most dangerous team we play."

GREEN BAY STAR REGGIE WHITE

*Randall Cunningham was supposed to be Minnesota's backup in 1998.
With help from Randy, he ended up winning the league's MVP award.*

Also, erased from the books—but still very much in the minds of the Packer defenders—were two long bombs Randy caught that were nullified by holding penalties. After the teams' second meeting, Brett Favre, the 1997 NFL Player of the Year, told Randy that he was a great player. Green Bay's superstar defensive lineman, Reggie White, said the difference between the two teams in 1998 was Randy.

In the season's 12th game, Randy was looking to administer a little payback. The Dallas Cowboys, in need of a receiver to pair with All-Pro Michael Irvin, had turned their backs on Randy on draft day. Now they had to face him without ace cornerback Deion Sanders, who was out with a sore foot. Randy murdered Dallas with three long touchdown catches in a 46–36 win.

The Vikings closed out the season with four more victories, including a Sunday night blowout of the Bears in which Randy had to step up and replace Reed and Carter, who were nursing injuries. He caught eight balls and scored three more touchdowns. Randy had at least one touchdown catch in each of the season's final seven games. His third score against the Bears established a new record for NFL rookies. "I knew I'd be

Randy gets his revenge on the Cowboys with a touchdown catch against Terry Billups. It was one of three TDs for Randy that day.

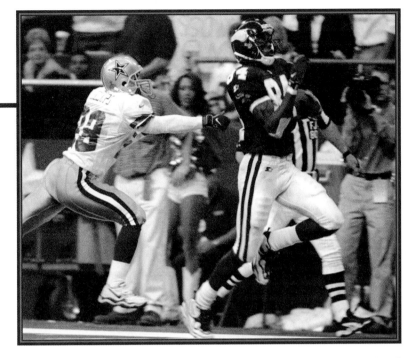

able to do the things I've always done," Randy insists.

In all, Randy found the end zone 17 times during the regular season. He and Carter each caught TDs in the last game against Tennessee, setting a new NFL mark for touchdowns by a receiving duo, with 28. The Vikings finished 15–1 (only the third team in history to do so) and set a new single-season record for total points, with 556.

In the playoffs, Randy scored twice more: once in a 41–21 win over the Cardinals and again in the NFC Championship against the Falcons. Unfortunately, the Vikings let that game slip away, as Atlanta won in overtime and advanced to the Super Bowl. It was a crushing blow to the Minnesota players and fans, who believed theirs was a team of destiny. Randy took it as hard as anyone.

pro stats

YEAR	GAMES	CATCHES	YARDS	YARDS/CATCH	TDs
1998	16	69	1,313	19.0	17

pro highlights

NFL Rookie of the Year 1998
Pro Bowl Selection 1998
Most TD Catches by a Rookie 1998

chapter 10

Millennium Man

"They brought me here to play football, score touchdowns, and put points on the board. That's what I'm focusing on, and hopefully I'll fulfill all my dreams."

— RANDY MOSS

After just one season, many of the same people who had condemned Randy as "uncoachable" or a "troublemaker" were showering him with praise. They now agree that he can be the first great receiver of the 21st century. People in the NFL are not fond of admitting their mistakes, especially when it comes to evaluating what makes young players tick. In Randy's case, however, most of his former doubters freely admitted that they had misjudged him. Once they saw his passion for the game, and his coolness under fire, they knew they had let a gem slip through their fingers.

Those who feared Randy might be a disruptive influence were also glad to see how completely he integrated himself into the team concept. When you have been 10 times better than your teammates your whole

Did You Know?

When teams began giving Randy more room to protect against the bomb, he perfected the "comeback route." Randy gets a defender backpedaling and then stops, spins, and steps back toward the quarterback for a bullet pass.

May I recommend the potato skins, ma'am? Randy and other Vikings served as waiters at a charity fund-raiser held at Planet Hollywood. Since coming to the NFL, Randy has become a big part of the community.

life, it can be hard adjusting to a situation where everyone is playing on the same level. Randy had no problem. He understood how he could make his teammates better, and how they could make *him* better. When he got the ball, he took care of business; when he did not, he never complained.

Many compare Randy to his hero, Jerry Rice. His ability to adjust to throws on-the-fly—to go into another "gear" just before catching the ball—does indeed resemble the 49ers' superstar. But Rice's specialty has always been catching a 10- or 15-yard pass and then slicing his way downfield. Randy's greatest gift is his ability to sprint halfway down the field and still catch anything near him. He outruns, outjumps, outstretches, and outdives defenders. And if that does not do the trick, he can make up a brand-new

Whenever Randy scores a touchdown in the Metrodome, he scales the back wall and leaps into the crowd.

move to get to the ball! As his teammates like to say, there is no such thing as a "Hail Mary" when you throw the ball to Randy—if the ball is close, he'll come up with it. He has also established himself as one of the top blockers at his position. Most coaches are happy if a receiver just puts a body on someone; Randy tries to flatten opponents. And when opponents flatten Randy, he never complains.

Randy surprised NFL observers in other ways. Contrary to his bad-boy image, he showed a lot of class on the field. When a defender made a good play and he and Randy went down, Randy would offer his hand to help the other man off the turf. And although he burned to make the teams that passed over him in the draft regret their decision, he did nothing to fire their players up. "I don't really talk back to anybody, or say anything in the papers about any team," he says.

By the season's last few weeks, it was clear what a unique player Randy was. He was a no-brainer for Rookie of the Year and was virtually assured a spot in the Pro Bowl. Did it go to his head? Hardly. Randy does not really think of himself as a superstar. "I just think of myself as a special player," he says. "A different type of player."

Of course, if Randy ever starts to get a big head, his teammates are sure to keep him humble. He might have been the most talented player on the Vikings in 1998, but he got the rookie treatment all season long. Randy had to fetch doughnuts for the veterans during Saturday morning meetings, and work the lights whenever the team gathered to watch videotape. In training camp, the veterans made him get up and sing his college fight song. Randy loved every minute of it.

NFL fans have loved every minute Randy has been in the league. They also have the sneaking suspicion that they have not yet seen how great Randy's speed really is. Believe it or not, a review of his catches from 1998 does not turn up a single play where he had to sprint all-out. Some say he gets downfield so fast that there is not a quarterback in the league who can take a five-step drop and then throw the ball beyond his grasp. Not even Randy knows how fast he can run.

Is he football's best receiver? Not yet, but the tools are there, as is the desire. Oddly enough, being called the NFL's top receiver is not as important to Randy as being the league's best *playmaker*. "I just want to make plays and help my team win," he says. "Especially away on the road. That's what motivates me—to hear fans screaming. It pushes me to make stuff happen."

Randy Moss taught the NFL an important lesson. What you see is not always what you get. And what you get can be a whole lot more than you expect. No one ever underestimated Randy's talents; they simply assumed that he was a bad guy—a cocky player who attracted trouble like a magnet. What they discovered was just the opposite. Randy is serious, respectful, and thoroughly devoted to the game. He learns fast and he listens. And despite his awesome individual talent, he always thinks of the team.

Randy has spent his entire life working toward the goal of playing in the NFL. Now he has arrived. Along the way he has made mistakes. He has paid dearly for them, and has endured more than his fair share of humiliation and prejudice along the way. Since he was a little kid, Randy has loved football. Now, finally, football is beginning to love him back.

Another season, another national magazine cover. There should be many more in Randy's future.

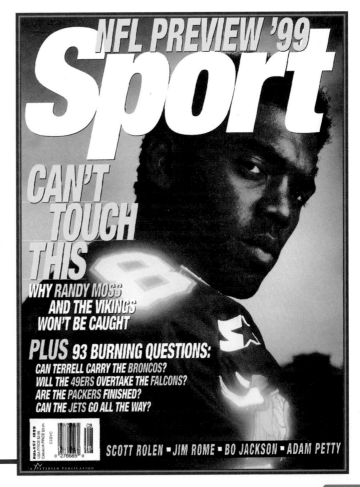

Index